I AM
Colour

Colour in Book for all Ages

33 Drawings
33 Affirmations

Penelope Smith

THE SANGREAL SODALITY PRESS
Johannesburg, Gauteng, South Africa

First edition 2017

Published by The Sangreal Sodality Press
74 Twelfth Street
Parkmore 2196
Gauteng
South Africa
Email: Jacobsang@gmail.com

email info@pennbrush.co.za

ISBN 978-0-620-77533-5

Also by Penelope Smith

72 Guiding Lights - Journey of self discovery

Selection of Books by Sangreal Sodality Press

Jacobus G. Swart: *The Book of Self Creation.* The Sangreal Sodality Press 2009
Jacobus G. Swart: *The Book of Sacred Names.* The Sangreal Sodality Press 2011
Jacobus G. Swart: *The Book of Seals & Amulets.* The Sangreal Sodality Press 2014.
Jacobus G. Swart: *The Book of Immediate Magic - Part 1.* The Sangreal Sodality Press 2015

Energy of Colour

We are colourful light fields of energy. The brightness of our colour and energy depends on our mood and well-being. These energy fields are unseen by most, we sense, rather than see them as they reflect our mood. Moods have always been associated with colour. For example; Blue we feel calm or down, Red we feel angry or powerful, Pink we are happy or loving, Yellow we feel clever or critical.

Colour is around us all the time, even if we cannot see it. The colour spectrum is there waiting to be revealed. We can see this when the sun shines through the raindrops creating a rainbow of colour that lights up the sky.

In the same way, this book is waiting for its colours to be revealed. When you choose a mood and colours to bring the pages to life, you will create the same kind of magic like sunshine on the clouds.

Colouring in can work on brightening our energy fields and our own rainbow. The brighter and more colourful we make our energy fields, the happier, healthier, positive and balanced we will be.

Black　　　　(I am Life)

Meaning: Colour of unity, grounding, the hidden, unknown, absorbs light
Represents: Power, elegance, mixed with another colours can strengthen that colour

Brown　　　　(I am Welcoming)

Meaning: Colour of stability, honesty, reliability, wholesome, protective, fertility.
Represents: Order, abundance, down to earth, structure and support.

Red　　　　(I am Desire)
Meaning: Colour of love and conflict, vibrant with life force and vigour.
Represents: Strength, passion, energy, courage, power, creativity.

Red/Orange　　(A merging of Desire and Creativity)

Orange　　　　(I am Creative)
Meaning: Colour of warmth, vital energy, stimulates creativity. thoughtfulness.
Represents: Courage, confidence, ambition, adventure, success, creative energies.

Orange/Yellow　(A merging of Creativity and Intuition)

Yellow　　　　(I am Intuitive)
Meaning: Colour of Wisdom, bright energy, clarity of thought, personal power.
Represents: Optimism, well-being, creativity, intellect, fun, logic, friendliness,

Yellow/Green (A merging of Intuition and Success)

Green (I am Successful)
Meaning: Colour of growth, renewal, connects lower self to higher self.
Represents: Hope, money, fertility, peace, rejuvenation, harmony, new beginnings.

Green/Blue (A merging of Success and Confidence)

Blue (I am Confident)
Meaning: Colour of communication, intuition, truth, honesty, calming.
Represents: Loyalty, intelligence, expansion, dedication, inner peace,

Blue/Purple (A merging of Confidence and Knowing)

Purple (I am Wise)
Meaning: Colour of the inner mind, universal consciousness, visions, understanding.
Represents: Luxury, devotion, wisdom, justice, fairness, integrity, idealistic.

Purple/Red (A merging of Wisdom and Desire)

Gold (I am Knowing)
Meaning: Colour of self-worth, standing in society, success,
Represents: Enlightenment, wisdom, intuitiveness, compassion.

Silver (I am Spirit)
Meaning: Colour of truth, emotions, mirrors negative or positive energy.
Represents: Intuition, imagination, inspiration, reflection, meditation, responsible,

Grey (I am Infinite)
Meaning: Colour of all possible possibilities, dynamic leadership.
Represents: self-respect, reliability, solid, stable, calming.

White (I am Pure)
Meaning: Colour of goodness, mind, spirit, perfection, peace, reflects light.
Represents: Purity, unity, transcendent, innocence, truth, protection, good over evil,

Colour mixing

Primary colours	=	Red, Yellow and Blue are the building blocks for all other colours.
Secondary colours	=	Orange, Green and Purple are created from two primary colours.
Tertiary colours	=	Red Orange, Yellow orange, Yellow Green, Green Blue, Blue Purple, Purple Red are created from a primary and secondary colour.

Warm colours	=	Red, Red Orange, Orange, Yellow Orange, Yellow, Yellow green.
Cool colours	=	Green, Green Blue, Blue, Blue Purple, Purple, Red Purple.

A Tint is created by adding white to a colour.
A Tone is created by adding grey to a colour.
A Shade is created by adding black to a colour.

Basic Techniques in colour matching

1	Complementary colours	=	Colours that compliment each other are on opposite sides of the colour wheel.
2	Split-complementary colours	=	Less contrast than the opposite colour as two colours are used either side of the complementary colour.
3	Triad colours	=	Three colours that are equally spaced around the colour wheel.
4	Analogous colours	=	Three colours that are next to each other on the colour wheel.
5	Square colour	=	Four colours equally spaced around colour wheel.

Colour wheels

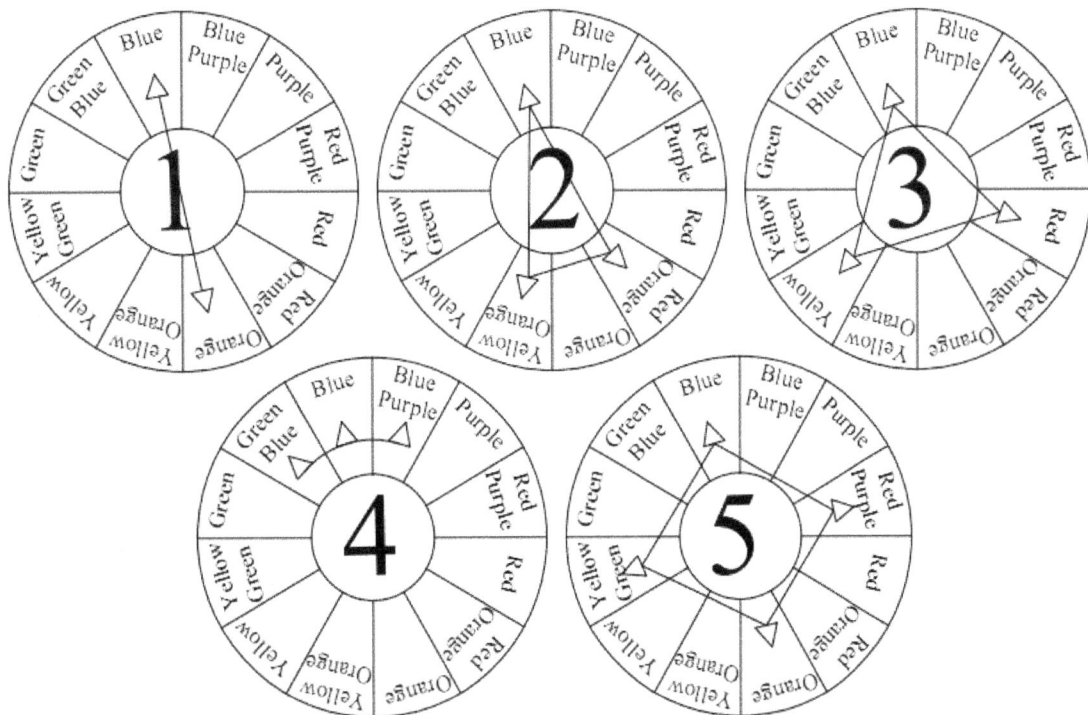

I AM
Colour

I AM
Loveable

I AM
Successful

I AM
Tolerant

I AM
Caring

I AM
Happy

I AM
Kindness

I AM
Wise

I AM
Wealthy

I AM
Healthy

I AM
Powerful

I AM
Creative

I AM
Beautiful

I AM
Grateful

I AM
Positive

I AM
Alive

I AM
Intuitive

I AM
Prosperous

I AM
Loyal

I AM
Dynamic

I AM
Amazing

I AM
Fearless

I AM
Focused

I AM
Relaxed

I AM
Inspiring

I AM
Brilliant

I AM
Vivacious

I AM
Perfect

I AM
Spiritual

I AM
Worthy

I AM
Light

I AM
Life

I AM
Knowing